THE SPINSTER

Robert Hichens

[ZHINGOORA BOOKS]

This edition is published by
Zhingoora Books.

I had arrived at Inley Abbey that afternoon, and was sitting at dinner with Inley and his pretty wife, whom I had not seen for five years, since the day I was his best man, when we all heard faintly the tolling of a church bell. Lady Inley shook her shoulders in a rather exaggerated shudder.

"Someone dead!" said her husband.

"It's a mistake to build a church in the grounds of a house," Lady Inley said in her clear, drawling soprano voice. "That noise gives me the blues."

"Whom can it be for?" asked Inley.

"Miss Bassett, probably," Lady Inley replied carelessly, helping herself to a bonbon from a little silver dish.

Inley started.

"Miss Sarah Bassett! What makes you think so?"

"Oh, while you were away in town she got ill. Didn't you know?"

"No," said Inley.

I could see that he was moved. His dark, short face had changed suddenly, and he stopped eating his fruit. Lady Inley went on crunching the bonbon between her little white teeth with all the enjoyment of a pretty marmoset.

"Influenza," she said airily. "And then pneumonia. Of course, at her age, you know—— By the way, what is her age, Nino?"

"No idea," said Inley shortly.

He was listening to the dim and monotonous sound of the church bell.

Lady Inley turned to me with the childish, confidential movement which men considered one of her many charms.

"Miss Bassett is, or was, one of those funny old spinsters who always look the same and always ridiculous. Dry twigs, you know. One size all the way down. Very little hair, and no emotions. If it weren't for the sake of cats, one would wonder why such people are born. But they're always cat-lovers. I suppose that's why they're so often called old cats."

She uttered a little high-pitched laugh, and got up.

"Don't be too long," she said to me carelessly as I opened the dining-room door for her. "I want to sing 'Ohé Charmette' to you.

"I won't be long," I answered, thinking what exquisite eyes she had.

She turned, and went out in her delicious, thin way. No wonder she had made skeletons the rage in London. When I came back to the dinner-table Inley was sitting with both his brown hands clenched on the cloth. His black eyes—inherited from his dead mother, who had been one of the Neapolitan aristocracy—were glittering.

"What is it, Nino?" I asked as I sat down.

We had been such intimate friends that even my five years' absence abroad had not built up a barrier between us.

"I wonder if it is Miss Bassett?" he said, looking at me earnestly.

"But was she a great friend of yours?" I said. "If Lady Inley's description of her is accurate, I can hardly imagine so."

"Vere doesn't know what she's saying."

"Then Miss Bassett———"

"Oh, she does look like that; dried up, unemotional, tame, English, even comic."

"The regular spinster, eh?"

"She looks it. But, damn it all, Vere has no business to say she has no emotions, to wonder why such people are born. But she doesn't know—Vere doesn't know."

His agitation grew, and was inexplicable to me. But I knew Inley, knew that he was bound to tell me what was on his mind. He could be reserved, but not with me. So I took a cigar, cut the end off it deliberately, struck a match, lighted it, and began to smoke in silence. He followed my example quickly, and then said:

"Vere talks like that, and, but for Miss Bassett, Vere would have been murdered two years ago."

I started, and dropped my cigar on the table.

"Murdered!"

"Yes; and I———"

He fixed his eyes on me, and put his hand up to his throat. Nino was half Neapolitan, and I saw a man being hanged. I picked up my cigar with a hand that slightly shook.

"But," I said, "I always thought Lady Inley and you were very happy together."

It sounded banal, even ridiculous, but I hardly knew what to say. I was startled. The tolling of the bell, too, was getting on my nerves.

"One doesn't write such things," he said. "You've been abroad for years."

"It's all right now?"

He nodded.

"I suppose so. Vere has never had the least suspicion."

He drew his chair closer to mine, and was about to go on speaking when the servants came in with the coffee.

"Who's the bell tolling for, Hurst?" he said to the butler.

"I couldn't say, my lord."

When the servants had gone Inley continued, at first in a calmer voice:

"Miss Bassett lived in the red cottage just beyond the gate of the South Lodge from time immemorial. You generally came to us in Scotland, I know, but I should think you must have seen her."

Suddenly a recollection flashed upon me—a recollection of a long, flat figure, a drab face, thin hair coming away from a wrinkled forehead under a mushroom hat, flapping, old-fashioned golden earrings.

"Not the person I used to call 'the Plank'?" I said.

"Did you?"

He thought for a moment.

"Yes; I believe you did-. I'd forgotten."

"She was always in church twenty minutes before the service began, and always dropped her hymn-book coming out if there were visitors in the Abbey pew!"

"Yes, yes; that's it. Miss Bassett is very nervous in little ways."

"I remember her now perfectly. And you say she——""

I looked at him, and hesitated.

"She saved Vere's life and, indirectly, mine. I'll tell you now we're together again at last. I shall never tell Vere."

He looked towards the windows, across which dark blue silk curtains were drawn, as if he could see the passing-bell swinging in the old square tower. Then he turned to me.

"You know how mad I was about Vere. It's always like that with me. Unless I'm stone I'm fire. After we were married I got even madder. Having her all to myself was like enchantment, and in Italy, too, my other native land."

I thought of Lady Inley's eyes.

"I can understand," I said.

"Of course, when we got back it had to be different. Friends came in, and she was run after and admired and written about. You know the publicity of life in modern London."

"City of public-houses and society spies."

"I bore it, because it's supposed to be the thing. And Vere rather likes it, somehow. So I let her have her fun, as long as it was fun. I didn't intend it should ever be anything else."

He frowned. When he did that, and his thick eyebrows nearly met, he looked all Italian.

"We did the usual things—Paris, Ascot, Scotland, and so on—till Vere had to lie up."

"Your boy?"

"Yes; Hugo came along. I was glad when that was over. I thought she was going to die. You knew Seymour Glynd?"

"Life Guards? Killed hunting a year ago?"

Inley nodded.

"He was a great deal with us soon after Hugo's birth. I thought nothing of it. I'd known the fellow all my life. But then one nearly always has."

He laughed bitterly.

"To cut that part short, two years ago in autumn we had Glynd staying with us down here for shooting. There were some others, of course—Mrs. Jack,

Bobbie Elphinton, and Lady Bobbie—but you know the lot."

"I did."

"Ah," he said, "you've been well out of it these years. Well, the shoot was to break up on a Friday, and I'd arranged to go to town that day with the rest. Vere didn't intend to come. She said she was feeling tired, and was going to have a Friday to Monday rest cure. That's the thing, you know, nowadays. You get a Swedish *masseuse* down to stay, and go to bed and drink milk. Vere had engaged a *masseuse* to come on the Friday night. On the Thursday, the day before we were all going to town, Glynd hurt his foot getting over a fence into a turnip field—at least I thought so."

He stopped.

"Everyone thought so, I believe—except, of course, Vere. I wonder if they did, though?" he added moodily. "Or whether I was the only—But what does it matter now? Glynd said he only wanted a couple of days' rest to be all right again, and asked me if he might stay on at the Abbey till the Monday. Of course I said 'Yes; if he wouldn't want a hostess.' Because Vere said to me, when she heard of it, that she must have her rest cure all the same. Glynd swore he'd be quite happy alone. So he stayed, and the rest of us came up to town on the Friday. Well, on the Saturday morning I was walking across the park when I met the Swedish *massense* who was to have gone down to Vere on the Friday night. I knew her, because Vere had often had her before in London. 'Hullo!' I said. 'You ought to be down at Inley Abbey with my wife.' 'No, my lord,' she said. 'Why not?' 'I've had a wire from Lady Inley not to go.' 'A wire!' I said. 'When did you get it?' 'On Thursday night, my lord.' 'You mean last night?' I said, thinking Vere must have changed her mind after we had left. 'No,' said the woman; 'on Thursday night, late.' Then I remembered that, after Glynd had hurt his foot and asked to stay, Vere had gone out alone for a drive in her cart, to get a last breath of air before the rest cure. She must have sent the telegram herself then. All of a sudden I seemed to understand a lot of things.'"

He had let his cigar out, and now he noticed that he had. He tossed it into the fire.

"I said, 'Good-morning' to the woman quite quietly, went back to the house, and told my man I shouldn't be at home that night."

He put his hand on my arm.

"I felt perfectly calm. Wasn't that strange?"

I nodded.

"There was a train from town reaching Ashdridge Station at nine o'clock at night. I took it. I didn't care to go to Inley Station, where everybody would know me, and wonder what I was up to. I didn't take any luggage. My man asked if he should pack, and I said 'No.' I didn't dine. I was at Pad-dington three-quarters of an hour before the train was due to start. At last it came in to the platform. Going down I read the evening papers just like any man going home from business. Soon after we got away from London I saw there was rain on the carriage windows. That seemed to me right. We were a little late at Ashdridge. It was still wet, and I had my coat collar turned up. I don't believe they recognised me there. I set out to walk to Inley."

"What did you mean to do?"

"I told you before."

I looked into his face, and believed him. Then I thought of Lady Inley's childish, delicate beauty, of her slightly affected manner, the manner of a woman who has always been spoilt, whose paths have been made very smooth. And here she was living, apparently happily, with a man who had deliberately travelled down in the night to kill her. How ignorant we are!

"You are condemning me," Inley said, with a touch of hot anger.

"I was only thinking———"

"Yes?"

"That we don't know each other much in the greatest intimacy."

"That's what I thought then."

He said that in a way which suddenly put me on his side. He must have seen the change in my feelings, for he went on, with his former unreserve:

"I walked fast in the dark. I didn't think very much, but I remember that all the trees—there's a lot of woodland, you know, between Ashdridge and Inley—seemed alive. Everything seemed to me to be alive that night. I've never had that sensation before or since."

I realised what the condition of the man had been when he said that, as if I were a doctor and a patient had told me the symptom which put me in possession of his malady.

"When I reached Inley it was late, and the long village street was deserted. There were lights in the inn and in the schoolmaster's house, but there were no people about. I got through without meeting a soul, and came on towards the gates of the Abbey."

"You meant to go into the house?"

"Yes. I was sure—somehow I was sure; but I intended to see before I acted, merely for my own justification. But I was quite sure, as if Vere herself had told me everything. Soon after I had got clear of the village I heard a sound of wheels behind me. I stood up against the hedge, and in a minute or two a fly passed me going slowly. I saw the driver's face. It wasn't a man from Inley. Evidently the fly had come from a distance. It was splashed with mud, and the horse looked tired. I followed it till it came to the turning just below Miss Bassett's cottage, where there's a narrow lane going to Charfield through the woods. It went a little way down this lane, and stopped. I waited at the turning. I could see the light from the lamps shining on the wet road, and in the circle of light the driver's breath. He bent down, and I saw him looking at a big silver watch. Then he put it back. But he didn't drive on. I knew what he was waiting for. Vere was going with—with Glynd. That was more than I had ever thought of, that she would go. I put my hand into my pocket, took out my revolver, and went on till I was close to the red cottage. By this time the rain had stopped. I came up to within a few yards of the Abbey gates, stood for a moment, and then returned till I was at the wicket of Miss Bassett's garden. It's bounded by a yew hedge, beyond which there is a path shaded by mulberry-trees. The hedge is low. The path is dark. It was a blackguardly thing to do, but I thought of nothing except myself, my wrong, and how I was to wipe it out. I opened the wicket, came into the path, and stood there under the mulberry-trees behind the hedge. Here I was in cover, and could see the road. I held my revolver in my hand, and waited. It never struck me that Miss Bassett might be up. I saw no light in the cottage, and I had a sort of idea that people like her went to bed at about eight. While I was standing there listening I felt something rub against my legs. It made me start. Then I heard a little low noise. I looked down, and there was a great cat holding up its tail and purring. Its pleasure was horrible to me. I pushed it away with my foot, but it came back, bending down its head, arching its back, and pressing against me. I was thinking what to do to get rid of it when I heard a shrill, husky voice call out:

"'Johnny—John-nee!'

"It was Miss Bassett. I held my breath, and pushed away the cat.

"'Johnny, Johnny—John-nee!' went the voice again.

"The cat wouldn't leave me. God knows why it wished to stay. I was determined to get rid of it, so I put the revolver down on the path, picked the cat up in my arms, and dropped it over the hedge into the road. Just as I had caught up the revolver again I was confronted by Miss Bassett. She had come in slippers up the path in the dark to look for her cat."

I uttered a slight exclamation.

Inley went on: "She had a handkerchief tied over her cap and under her chin, and a small lantern in her hands, on which she wore black mittens. I can see her now. We stood there on the path for a minute staring at each other without a word. The light from the lantern flickered over the revolver, and I saw Miss Bassett look down at it."

He stopped, poured out a glass of water, and drank it off like a man who has been running.

"Didn't she show surprise—fear?" I asked.

"Not a bit. Women are so extraordinary, even old women who've never been in touch with life, that I'm certain now she understood directly her eyes fell on the revolver."

"What did she do?"

"After a minute she said: 'Lord Inley, I'm looking for my cat. Have you seen him?'

"'Yes,' I said; 'he's run into the house.'

"It was a lie, but I wanted her to go in. I had slipped the revolver back into my pocket, and tried to assume a perfectly simple, natural air. I fancied it would be very easy to impose on Miss Bassett when I heard her question. It sounded so innocent, as if the old lady was full of her pet. I even thought, perhaps, she had not known what the revolver was when she looked at it.

"'Did he run into the house?' she said, still looking at me from under her wrinkled eyelids.

"'Yes; when you came out. He was here on the path with me. You called "Johnny!" and he ran off there between the mulberry-trees.'

"All the time I was speaking to her I had an eye to the road, and my ears were listening like an Indian's when he puts his head to the ground to hear the pad of his enemy.

"Miss Bassett stood there quietly for a moment as if she were considering something. She looked prim. I remember that even now—prim as a caricature. It was only a moment, but it seemed to me an hour. 'If they should come,' I thought, 'while she is out here!' The sweat came out all over my face with impatience—an agony of impatience. I longed to take the old lady by the shoulders, push her into the cottage, lock her in, and be alone, able to watch the bit of road from the Abbey gates to the wicket. But I could do nothing. I was obliged to repress every sign of agitation. It was devilish."

He got up with a sudden jerk from his chair, and stood by the fire. Even the telling of that moment had set beads of moisture on his square, low forehead.

"At last she spoke again.

"'I wonder if you'd mind coming in for a minute to help me see if Johnny really is in the house?' she said.

"I don't know what I should have done—refused, I believe, refused her with an oath, for I began to feel mad; but just at that instant up came the cat once more, purring like fury, and lifting up his tail. He made straight for me, and began to rub himself against my legs again.

"'Oh!' said Miss Bassett, 'there he is! Naughty Johnny, naughty boy! Lord Inley, perhaps you'd be so good as just to lif t him up and put him inside the door for me. I always have such a job to get him to come in of a night. He likes hunting in the woods. Doesn't he, the naughty Johnny?'

"'Now's my chance to get rid of her!' I thought.

"I bent down, picked the cat up, and went along the path towards the cottage, Miss Bassett following close behind me. The cat was an immense beast, awfully heavy, and just as I turned out of the yew path to go up to the cottage door he began struggling to get away, and scratching. I held on to him, but it wasn't easy, and I got my hand torn before I dropped him down inside the little hall. Away he ran, towards the kitchen, I suppose. Miss Bassett was very grateful, but I cut her gratitude short.

"'Very glad to have been able to help you,' I said. 'Good-night.'

"'Good-night, Lord Inley,' she said.

"I thought her voice sounded a little bit odd when she said that, and I just glanced at her funny old face, lit up by the lantern she was holding in one mittened hand. She didn't look at me this time as she had in the garden. Then I went out, and she immediately shut the door.

"'Thank God!' I thought, and I hurried to the wicket. I didn't dare stay in the garden now. Seeing her had made me realise my blackguardism in coming in at all, considering my reason. I resolved to hide in the field at the corner where the road turns off to Charfield. As I opened the wicket, instinctively I put my hand into my pocket for my revolver."

He bent down, looking full into my eyes.

"It wasn't there."

"Miss Bassett!" I exclaimed.

"In a moment I realised that Miss Bassett must have grasped the situation; that her asking me to carry in her cat was a ruse, and that while the beast was struggling between my hands she must have stolen the revolver from behind. I say I knew that, and yet even then, when I thought of her look, her manner, the sort of nervous old thing she was, I couldn't believe what I knew. Then I remembered her voice when she said 'Good-night' to me in the passage, her eyes looking down instead of at me, and that she was only holding the lantern in one hand, whereas in the garden she was using two. She must have had the revolver in her other hand concealed in the folds of her dress. I ran back to the cottage door, and knocked—hard. Not that I thought she'd open. I knew she wouldn't, but she did directly. I could hardly speak. I was afraid of myself just then. At last I said:

"'Miss Bassett, you know what I want.'

"'You can't have it,' she said, looking straight at me.

"I kept quiet for a second, then I said:

"'Miss Bassett, I don't think you know that you're running into danger.' For I felt that there was danger for her then if she went against me. She knew it, too, perhaps better than I did. I saw her poor old hands, all blue veins, beginning to tremble.

"'You can't have it, Lord Inley,' she repeated.

"There wasn't the ghost of a quiver in her voice.

"'I must, I will!' I said, and I made a movement towards her—a violent movement I know it was.

"But the old thing stood her ground. Oh, she was a gallant old woman.

"'Do what you like to me,' she said. 'I'm old. What does it matter? She's young.'

"Then I knew she understood.

"'You've seen them together!' I said. 'Since I went!'

"She wouldn't say. Not a word. I was mad. I forgot decency, everything. I took her. I searched her for the revolver. I searched her roughly—God forgive me. She trembled horribly, but never said a word. It wasn't on her. She must have hidden it somewhere in that moment when she was alone in the cottage. That was another ruse to keep me searching in there while— But I saw it almost directly. I broke away, and rushed out and down the road. Something seemed to tell me they had passed. I got into the lane that leads to Charfield. The fly was gone. Then, all of a sudden, I felt perfectly calm. I turned, and went up to the Abbey gates. I knocked them up at the lodge. The keeper came out. When he saw me he said:

"'You, my lord! However did you know?'

"'Go on!' I said. 'Know what?'

"'About Master Hugo?'

"I didn't say one way or the other.

"'The doctor says it's a bitter bad quinsy, but there's just a chance. Her ladyship's nearly mad. It only came on a few hours ago quite sudden.'

"I went up to the Abbey, and found Vere by the child's bed. She looked flushed, and was breathing hard, as if she had just been running."

He stopped, and took out his cigar-case.

"Running!" I said.

"She had parted finally from Glynd in front of Miss Bassett's cottage," he said. "He told me that afterwards."

There was a moment's silence. Then he spoke more calmly.

"I went up to town when the child was safe, and had it out with Glynd. They had meant to go that night. It was the boy who stopped them and they took it as a judgment. You know how women are. Glynd swore she was stopped in time. You understand?"

"Yes."

"He didn't lie to me."

"And your wife?"

"I never spoke of it to her. I saw her with the boy, and—well, I saw her with the boy, and what she was to him when he was close to death."

His voice went for a moment. Then he added:

"I told her I'd had a presentiment Hugo was ill. She believed me, I think. If not, she's kept her secret."

Just then the dining-room door opened, and Lady Inley put in her pretty head.

"Are you never coming?" she said with her little childish drawl.

I got up, and went towards her.

"By the way, Nino," she added, "the bell was for poor, funny old Miss Bassett. What will her cat do, I wonder?"

As I followed her towards the drawing-room I heard Inley's voice mutter behind me:

"*Requiescat in Pace.*"

End of the book.